Original title:
Rhyme in Zero-G

Copyright © 2025 Creative Arts Management OÜ
All rights reserved.

Author: Penelope Hawthorne
ISBN HARDBACK: 978-1-80567-778-9
ISBN PAPERBACK: 978-1-80567-899-1

Verses Beyond the Veil

Floating up high, a giggle takes flight,
Spinning in circles, what a silly sight!
Tangled in stardust, we dance and we sway,
Gravity's holding its breath, in dismay.

Bouncing off walls, we land on our head,
Laughter erupts, even up in our bed!
Cosmic confetti rains down with a cheer,
A party in space that's absurdly near.

Sipping on space juice, it splashes and flies,
We catch it in cups made of hopes and of pies.
Galactic jokes float like comets in spree,
Every punchline explodes, what glee!

Friends in the void, our antics collide,
Chasing lost socks on a whimsical ride.
Planets all chuckle, the universe grins,
In the great, vast cosmic, where nonsense begins.

Weightless Waltzes

In a ship that floats up high,
We twirl and spin, oh my,
A dance with no ground to hold,
Where laughter's worth more than gold.

With floating snacks in a line,
A cosmic feast, oh so divine,
Each bite that drifts away,
Makes dinner feel like play.

Pulsars and Poetry

A neutron star with a beat,
Makes everyone tap their feet,
Words bounce around the room,
In a cosmic, rhythmic bloom.

We scribble verses with glee,
In an orbit, wild and free,
With quarks that giggle and sway,
Poetry's here to play!

Nebulous Notes

In clouds of dust, we sing,
As twinkling stars take wing,
Melodies drift, oh what fun,
Chasing echoes one by one.

With cosmic chords all aglow,
We harmonize in a flow,
Galactic giggles fill the air,
Who knew space could be so rare?

In the Silence of Space

In quiet voids where echoes hide,
We joke and jest, we glide with pride,
Absence of sound, yet joy abounds,
As laughter twirls in merry rounds.

With floating friends, we take a chance,
An absurd and weightless dance,
In silence, we find our delight,
With humor soaring into the night.

Starlight Stories

In a rocket ship, we laugh and glide,
Floating snacks and giggles inside.
The astronaut puppy chases its tail,
While space whales sing a goofy wail.

Meteors dodge like a game of catch,
Bouncing off planets with an electric batch.
We tell jokes to Martians, and they just beam,
In this weightless world, we all share a dream.

Beyond the Blue Horizon

Starfish swim through cosmic seas,
Wearing silly hats, dancing with ease.
Galaxies twirl in a wobbly hug,
While aliens juggle a floating bug.

We ride the rings of Saturn's flair,
Pretending we're clouds without a care.
The Milky Way laughs, it's quite a sight,
In an endless dance through the starry night.

Orbital Poetry

Zero-G poetry takes a flight,
Words bounce around, and what a sight!
Comets throw parties, they light up the sky,
Snapping selfies as they zoom by.

Black holes have jokes, they twist your mind,
But we're all here, just having a kind.
Gravity is shy, it won't come to play,
We'd rather float and laugh all day.

Antigravity Ballads

In a space lounge, we strum and croon,
Melodies swirl like a spinning balloon.
Aliens tap dance on floating chords,
While Martian cats play with laser swords.

Balloons drift by with a squeaky cheer,
Giggling voices fill the atmosphere.
Songs in the cosmos, so bright and bold,
In this buoyant world, adventure unfolds.

Serene Space Syllables

Floating high, in cosmic haze,
Words turn silly, in a playful maze,
No gravity to keep them tight,
They dance around, in pure delight.

Jokes are tossed like shooting stars,
Laughter echoes, near and far,
In this realm, where dreams collide,
Witty thoughts take their wild ride.

Celestial Narrative

Once a comet, bright and bold,
Told a tale that time retold,
Of space squirrels with acorn hats,
Chasing rays and playful spats.

Asteroids giggled in a line,
Poking fun like it's divine,
In this void where quirk's the game,
Every whisper fuels the flame.

A Distant Chorus

Stars hum tunes, a jovial mix,
Planets join in, a cosmic fix,
Aliens sing with silly glee,
As moonbeams twirl like they're carefree.

Saturn's rings clap to the beat,
Meteors stomp with happy feet,
In this choir of the bright and weird,
Every chuckle's loudly cheered.

Poetic Pulsation

Galaxies bounce in rhythmic sway,
While space cats dart, in a feline play,
Orbiting jokes, around they spin,
Silly bubbles float, let the fun begin.

Neon comets flash with cheer,
Lunar laughs, to all who hear,
In this vast, bewildering space,
Joyful verses find their place.

Zero-Gravity Haikus

Floating like a feather,
Socks launch into orbit,
Chasing them is hard,
Laughter fills the air.

Twinkling stars above,
Coffee drips like moonbeams,
A splash in space? Yes!
Oops, it's now a dream.

Hang on to your snacks,
They glide away from hands,
Just like lost wishes,
In weightless wonderlands.

Celestial Caress

In the cosmic dance,
We twirl with glee and grace,
Stars tickle our toes,
In this endless chase.

Asteroids declare war,
On what we call the ground,
We giggle and we spin,
In this joyful bound.

Galaxies collide,
With a wink and a smile,
Gravity's just a joke,
So let's float a while.

Dancing in the Vacuum

Waltzing with a smile,
My hair defies the norm,
Floating through the void,
With a weathered charm.

Tickling the planet,
With a fluffy cloud,
Earth's a distant thought,
Can we sing out loud?

Spinning somersaults,
Through the endless night,
Stars laugh with just glee,
What a glorious sight.

Lunar Lullabies

Singing to the moon,
While comets drift on by,
No beds, just soft dreams,
In a soft, starry sky.

Crickets chirp in space,
With a tinkling sound,
We sway with the tides,
Which are playful and round.

Sleepy in the stars,
With Milky Way embrace,
We laugh through the night,
In this grand, cozy place.

Lyric Drift

In a ship that does twirl,
My words swirl and whirl,
Floating high with a grin,
Each phrase wants to spin.

Lost socks and old hats,
Dance with cosmic chitchats,
Gravity? It's a prank!
Words float in the dank.

A comet's tail swings wide,
Rhymes on a joyride,
Quips leap through the air,
Like ducks without care.

The stars giggle loud,
As I bounce off a crowd,
Speech takes a weird dive,
In this verse, we arrive!

Galaxy of Letters

Twinkling up in the dark,
Letters chase like a lark,
A-B-C do a jig,
Underneath a big fig.

Word planets spin and dart,
Spelling fun with great art,
With each loop and wild flip,
The alphabet starts to slip.

Cosmic hiccups arise,
Surprising with weird ties,
Puns floating on the breeze,
Like a cat with new keys.

Scribbles swirl in the night,
Filling voids with delight,
Crafting joy light as air,
Galactic giggles to share!

Sonic Skyfall

When sound waves take a leap,
They bounce and giggle deep,
Up above there's a song,
That wiggles all night long.

Sound bubbles burst like fun,
Each note's a little run,
Through the cosmos they race,
In a wild, spacey chase.

Chirps and chirrs fill the void,
With laughter unalloyed,
The echoes twist and shout,
In zero-G, there's no doubt.

A meteoric laugh track,
Twirling on its own back,
Out in this splendid sprawl,
The music just can't fall!

Moonlit Melodies

Under a glowing sphere,
Silly songs start to cheer,
With each note in the sky,
A giggle lets out a sigh.

Whispers float on moonbeams,
Bouncing off twinkling dreams,
Puns and quirks full of zest,
In this place, all are blessed.

Harmony skips in flight,
Bringing joy, pure delight,
As the shadows take shape,
In this musical tape.

Stars hum to the sweet tune,
Dancing round like a loon,
In this lunar embrace,
Laughter finds its right place!

Verses in the Void

In space, I lost my shoe,
It floated right past you!
My socks are now a fleet,
Adrift in cosmic heat.

A sandwich spun away,
It danced in bright array.
With jelly on my face,
I laughed in empty space.

Orbiting a moon,
I tried to hum a tune.
But gravity's a tease,
And I'm lost in the breeze.

The stars are not so wise,
They twinkle with surprise.
As I flip and twirl,
In this wild space-furl!

Ethereal Euphony

Floating like a feather,
My lunch is light as leather.
A pickle takes a spin,
An acrobat's sweet grin.

With cows in a twirl,
A cowgirl gives a whirl!
In the vacuum's embrace,
We dance in rapid race.

The comet's got a grin,
Says 'Join the twirly spin!'
We laugh as we collide,
In our zooming pride.

My hair defies all laws,
As zero-G gives pause.
It floats like soft confetti,
In this goofy jetty!

Cosmic Chords

Plucking stars like strings,
And joy is what it brings.
A melody of laughs,
As cosmic music wafts.

Zero-G guitar,
Playing notes from afar.
The blender plays along,
In our galactic song.

A jellybean takes flight,
It's a colorful sight.
With laughter mixed in air,
We float without a care.

An asteroid's a drum,
Oh, what a silly hum!
We jam through stellar light,
In fun we find our flight.

Stellar Soliloquies

I talk to the bright sun,
While circling 'round for fun.
It winks and waves goodbye,
As I float up high.

Chasing comets at night,
In a chase that's just right.
My shadow's gone to play,
Out here it's a ballet.

With planets as my stage,
I unleash cosmic rage.
A dance of light and sound,
While I spin round and round!

Giggles echo in space,
With stars keeping the pace.
In this floating bazaar,
Who knew I'd go so far?

Celestial Echoes

In space, I dropped my sandwich here,
It floated past without a care.
A pickle rolled as if in glee,
Said, "Come join me—let's float free!"

The stars above wear silly hats,
They twinkle bright like dancing cats.
A comet zoomed with a silly grin,
"Catch me if you can!" it did spin!

The moon, it laughed—a chuckle low,
"I'm the king of lunar show!"
With craters wide that look like eyes,
It winks at me—a big surprise.

In cosmic games, we play all day,
With meteors that swerve and sway.
I'll race a rocket, let's see who wins,
But I'll just laugh, for fun begins.

Weightless Whispers

A feather floats, a graceful dance,
In zero gravity, it's pure chance.
I tried to catch it, oh what fun,
But it zips away, just like a gun!

Chatting with stars, they tell me tales,
Of space-fish swimming with comet trails.
"Tap-dancing aliens" they claim to see,
With shiny boots, all full of glee!

The planets giggle, their orbits wide,
As I drift along with cosmic pride.
I swear I heard the sun declare,
"I'm the hottest here—beyond compare!"

And so we twirl in this vast expanse,
Where laughter echoes, and bodies prance.
With each new twist, a joke is spun,
In this merry void, there's endless fun!

Orbiting Words

Words spin round like satellites,
In laughter's grip, they take their flights.
A pun drifts by on a solar breeze,
Tickling the stars with playful tease.

I met a quasar with quite the jest,
It said, "Why not? Just float and rest!"
With a radiant smile and a wink so bright,
We bounced around, what a silly sight!

An asteroid wearing a goofy face,
Danced in circles, what a clumsy grace!
"I'm just here for a cosmic cheer,
To make you laugh, that's why I'm here!"

So in this orbit, joy's our guide,
With playful quips, we twist and slide.
In the galaxy's arms, we happily roam,
With words afloat, we've found a home!

Nebula Narratives

In swirling gas, the stories bloom,
Like cotton candy in the gloom.
Each tale of laughter, light, and cheer,
Drifts through the stars, so crystal clear.

A rogue asteroid told me a pun,
That brought forth laughter like the sun.
"Why did the black hole laugh so loud?
It had a joke that's really proud!"

A swirling cloud shared secrets wide,
Of interstellar whims its tides did ride.
With shooting stars chuckling bright,
They filled the void with pure delight.

So as we float in this cosmic tide,
With nebulae where joy can't hide,
We'll spin our tales, in gales of night,
Creating laughter in starlit flight.

Lyrics of the Universe

In space so vast, we float around,
With silly laughs, no solid ground.
A sandwich flies, oh what a sight,
We munch and giggle in pure delight.

Stars twinkle bright, like jokes in light,
We dance in orbit, joy takes flight.
A cat in a suit, a dog with a tie,
Floating through bubbles, oh me, oh my!

Galaxies spin, like a dance-off show,
We whirl and twirl, together we go.
With comets that dive, and meteors that spring,
We sing with the cosmos, oh what a fling!

So grab a space joke, it's time for a cheer,
In this funny world, there's nothing to fear.
With laughter and love, our spirits do soar,
In the universe's arms, forever more.

Twinkling Tones

A distant star, with a wink and a wink,
Shouted a tune, made us stop and think.
Planets chimed in with a comical beat,
As laughter echoed through cosmic heat.

The moon did a dance, all cheery and round,
While asteroids wobbled, falling to ground.
We giggled and spun on this glorious ride,
With a galactic orchestra, our laughter is our guide.

Shooting stars raced, each one a jest,
Who could be first, in this cosmic quest?
With silly sounds and playful vibes,
In this weightless wonder, joy resides.

So let's celebrate with zero-gravity cheer,
Where every tickle brings a grin ear to ear.
With playful tones, we frolic and play,
In the starlit laughter, we'll float away.

The Rhythm of Infinity

In a twisty loop, we jump and spin,
Gravity's gone; let the fun begin!
A bouncy ball floats, a curious sight,
As we giggle and dance in the cosmic night.

The planets hum a tuneful song,
While we flip and twirl, nothing feels wrong.
A comet trips, and we burst with glee,
In sync with the stars, we're totally free!

Saturn's rings rattle, a jingle so bright,
As we bounce like bunnies through the starry night.
Uranus chuckles, with a wink and a wink,
In this endless fun, we never rethink.

So join in the giggles, in this grand expanse,
With every silly move, we take a chance.
In this rhythm of joy, we find our way,
In the fabric of space, we dance and sway.

Cosmic Verses

A star named Blink, said, 'What's up, guys?'
With a laugh like thunder that lights up the skies.
We tumbled and twirled in a friendly embrace,
In the cosmic ballet, we found our place.

A planet once pranked, painted polka dots,
Creating confusion, oh, what funny spots!
The sun gave a grin, a beam of pure cheer,
Lighting our hearts, as we floated near.

With aliens juggling and waving hello,
We spun in a whirlwind, putting on a show.
They tossed us some comets, round like a pie,
Laughing so hard, we almost could fly!

So gather your friends and come take a ride,
In this wacky universe, laughter won't hide.
With joyful delight and zero-gravity fun,
We'll dance in the stars, till the day is done.

Orbiting Imagery

In space, the snacks just float around,
Potato chips defy the ground.
A sandwich spins, it finds its way,
And jelly drips, it starts to play.

Sipping soda takes some skill,
As bubbles bounce, oh what a thrill!
A cosmic dance, we sway and glide,
In the vastness, we take a ride.

Giggles echo through the void,
A rubber duck? We've been joyed!
It quacks and flips, a silly sight,
As starlight bathes us in pure light.

With each loop, we share our glee,
Weightless fun, just you and me.
In this realm of endless flight,
Let's laugh and play all through the night.

Driftwood of Dreams

Upon a beam, a comet flies,
With squeaky wheels and flashy ties.
It's pumping tunes, a wacky beat,
While gravity's lost, life is sweet.

Our hats are floating with great flair,
A pear-shaped ball bounces in air.
We tickle moons and tease the stars,
Performing tricks with candy bars.

A space-time picnic brings delight,
As we devour cupcakes in flight.
With whipped cream clouds, we cheer and shout,
In this weird place, we twist about.

We build a fort from cosmic dust,
And dress the asteroids with rust.
In driftwood dreams, we find our place,
With laughter echoing through the space.

Aetherial Anthems

With laughter ringing, in the air,
An alien joins us, full of flair.
He dances 'round on lazy beams,
And croons to us about his dreams.

Our helmets bounce, a playful cheer,
As echoes swirl, we draw near.
Each verse we sing drifts past the stars,
In this odd realm, we're cosmic czars.

The planets bop, they roll and spin,
With every note, we laugh and grin.
A drum of meteors keeps the time,
And jellyfish join in with a chime.

As stardust rains, we craft our song,
Together in space, we all belong.
With aetherial vibes, we sing out loud,
In this whimsical world, where dreams are proud.

The Space Between Lines

In the gaps of space, we float with ease,
Avoiding comets, weaving through trees.
A quirky dance on nothingness,
With each step back, we feel the press.

The puns take flight, they soar so high,
Like pizza boxes escaping the pie.
A jovial grin upon our face,
We navigate this wacky place.

Invisible bounds cannot confine,
A giggle's drift, a silly sign.
In the bounds of void, we break the mold,
Our jokes shine bright, a tale retold.

So let's embrace the silly ride,
In the cosmos vast, let fun abide.
In the space between, we find our cheer,
In laughter's orbit, we hold so dear.

Ethereal Echoes

In space, I trip on floating socks,
I laugh while dodging starry flocks.
A comet sneezes, sends me spinning,
In weightless giggles, joy's beginning.

Gravity's lost in this vast dome,
Jokes are bouncing, far from home.
Every chuckle hangs in the air,
Like planets playing truth or dare.

Bubbles float with secret glee,
Tickling astronauts, oh so free.
A moonbeam winks, oh what a sight,
In laughter's grasp, the stars ignite.

So come and dance with cosmic glee,
On trails of laughter, just you and me.
Let humor guide our precious flight,
In this vast void, joy ignites bright.

Nebula of Words

Words are drifting, swirls of fun,
In space, we play, a race to run.
Floating phrases, funny and light,
Bouncing softly, reaching new height.

I told a joke to asteroid Joe,
He laughed so hard, he started to glow.
Galaxies giggle, twinkling with cheer,
A cosmic chorus that's loud and clear.

Lasers dance with playful zest,
In this expanse, we're quite the jest.
A supernova's laughter rings,
As stars debate the silliest things.

On cosmic waves, we surf and grin,
While black holes pull us in for the win.
Write a tale on a comet's tail,
In this nebula, we'll never fail!

Poetry in Motion

With each float, a whimsy twist,
In zero gravity's quirky mist.
I pen a line that swirls like gas,
A funny thought that's bound to pass.

Floating pens and goofy dreams,
Make poetry burst at the seams.
Lines collide like shooting stars,
Creating laughter that's truly ours.

The Milky Way plays hide and seek,
As cosmic giggles dance and peek.
Astronauts slip on starlit dew,
In this merry chaos, we break through.

So spin with words in joyous flight,
As laughter sparkles through the night.
A floating stanza, light and free,
In motion, we find our jubilee.

Celestial Whispers

In cosmic voids, we whisper tales,
Of floating fish and shooting snails.
Stars chuckle softly, twinkling bright,
In this endless dance, we feel the light.

Asteroids play hopscotch above,
While comets chase a puppy love.
Galactic giggles, echoes of mirth,
In every silence, we find our worth.

With a wink from the sun, we tease the moon,
Tickling shadows with a silly tune.
Shooting stars, a wink to say,
Life's a jest in the Milky Way.

So let's float high with laughter's crest,
In this boundless sky, we are blessed.
With every whisper, joy's decree,
In celestial play, we're ever free.

Unbound Ballad

In a ship where gravity's gone,
Astronauts dance till the break of dawn.
They float with glee, a wobbly waltz,
Their laughter echoes in cosmic vaults.

With snacks that drift and drinks that swirl,
One lost a chip, it twirled and twirled.
They chase it down, a game of tag,
In zero-g, even chips can brag.

A cat that leaps from wall to wall,
In weightlessness, it feels so tall.
It lands on heads, a furry surprise,
As giggles burst out, oh, how time flies!

Space suits shining, helmets aglow,
With silly faces, putting on a show.
As laughter rings through the vast expanse,
In the void, they find their balance and dance.

Ether's Embrace

Floating high in a sea of stars,
A crew debates their favorite cars.
One says, 'Mine's a rocket, sleek and bright,'
Another quips, 'Bring snacks for the flight!'

The captain sighs, 'Please keep it straight,
We're floating here, it's getting late.'
Yet laughter bubbles like soda pop,
In this wacky place, can't let it stop!

A blender spins, a smoothie in tow,
Fruit flying high, a fruity show.
Strawberries drift like comets near,
In this dance, there's nothing to fear.

With each slip and slide of space's light,
They find pure joy in the starry night.
With goofy grins and silly schemes,
They float through life, living their dreams.

Spacebound Sonnets

Two astronauts float in a tangled mess,
Wrestling with bags, it's quite the excess.
One spins around in a baggy suit,
Laughing so hard, he lost his route.

The other groans, 'Hold on, don't flee!'
But gravity's lost, they're free as can be.
With each twist and turn, they create a sight,
In this endless dance, everything feels right.

Bananas drift, no need for a table,
Making smoothies? Oh, if they're able!
With splashes of fruit in this carefree plight,
The cosmos is ripe, and everything's light.

So they toast with their cups of floating goo,
In the expanse of space, there's much fun to pursue.
With silly antics and snacks on parade,
In the grand dance of stars, a laugh is made.

Interstellar Lyrics

A rocket ship zooms past a stellar view,
Inside, a band plays a cosmic tune.
With guitars that float and drums on the wall,
They jam in the void, not worried at all.

The singer flips, nearly lost in the air,
But finds his footing with a brotherly care.
'Hey, let's rewrite this song on the fly,
Let's see how many notes can reach for the sky!'

As meteors flash, they improvise fast,
With beats that thrive, this moment won't last.
They whirl around, each note a delight,
In the vacuum, their music ignites.

So sing along, let the starlight inspire,
In this funny space, feel the musical fire.
With laughter and tunes, the universe sings,
In this dance of the void, joy always springs.

Orbiting Echoes

In a ship that's spinning round,
My breakfast floats without a sound.
A bagel here, a toast there,
It's a feast in cosmic air.

Laughing at my floating spoon,
It dances to a silent tune.
We're the clowns in space's game,
Chasing crumbs, it's quite the fame.

Our jokes drift through the endless black,
With giggles echoing, no way back.
The stars are bright, the puns are too,
In this vastness, we'll share a brew.

As I trip on gravity's prank,
I tumble through a shining bank.
A cosmic tumble, don't you know?
I'll write a book on how to float low.

Poems Among the Stars

A rocket ride to nowhere fast,
With poems that will surely last.
In starlit ink, my thoughts take flight,
While aliens giggle at our plight.

Each verse is like a comet's tail,
Funnier than a fishy tale.
We pen our dreams with zero fuss,
In the dark, it's quite a plus.

Spinning tales of cosmic woes,
Where every line a mystery shows.
A laugh among the endless skies,
Creativity that never lies.

So here we float, a silly crew,
With rhymes that dance like morning dew.
Among the stars, we'll make our mark,
In a universe that's bright and stark.

Galactic Melodies

In the void, our laughter sings,
As we sample space's tasty things.
With moon pies floating by our side,
We munch and crunch in joyful pride.

Our shenanigans, a cosmic tune,
Jokes echo softly; they strut and swoon.
Like satellites, our thoughts collide,
Finding humor as we slide.

A dancing star with a twinkling smile,
Mocks our gravity for a while.
In this weightless funny show,
We're comedians on cosmic flow.

So let's toast to the infinite jest,
With galactic giggles, we are blessed.
Each verse a note from far away,
In the melody of our play.

Nebulae of Narrative

In a cloud of colors, we take flight,
Our stories swirl through voided night.
With every twist and comic spin,
We'll surely find the laughs within.

Floating words in vibrant hue,
As we chart our course anew.
Every verse a stellar quirk,
In the universe, we'll boldly lurk.

With space hat on, my pen will glide,
Creating tales from cosmic tide.
Each punchline born from starlit dust,
In vastness, our humor is a must.

As meteors dash across the scene,
We'll dance through tales, both bright and green.
In nebulae, we'll dream and write,
With grins that shine like stars at night.

Floating Verses

In space, my socks just float away,
I chase them down, but they won't stay.
My cereal dances in the air,
As I try to sip from my floating chair.

Yet here I am, a happy fool,
With breakfast treats that break the rule.
My spoon does flips, it takes a dive,
Who knew that gravity could come alive?

I whistle tunes as I glide around,
While astronauts laugh, they make no sound.
The stars all wink, they know the game,
In this great void, we're all the same.

So let's embrace this weightless jest,
In cosmic fun, we feel our best.
With every giggle, we float and spin,
Who knew space travel could feel like a win?

Cosmic Cadence

A comet zooms past with a funny face,
Twirling through stars in a silly race.
Space dust giggles, it twirls around,
As we bounce off walls, no need for sound.

The moon has jokes, I hear it chuckle,
While planets spin, they stifle a chuckle.
My buddy's hair is in wild disarray,
As we float through the night, in a goofy ballet.

A meteor shower, what a sight,
Oh wait, it's just my snacks in flight!
I dodge the chips as they zoom and whirl,
In a galactic dance, oh what a swirl!

Zero gravity brings a light-hearted cheer,
Each twist and turn, we shed a tear.
In this starry realm, we can't help but grin,
Who knew that space could be so much fun?

Starlit Stanzas

Stars, they giggle, as comets tease,
I reach for one, but they just wheeze.
Floating here, my shoes take flight,
Chasing dreams in the deep of night.

Galactic donuts drift and roll,
While I slip on, a sugary goal.
My friend spins fast, can't help but laugh,
As space turns silly, do the math!

We play tag with the satellites,
While floating jellybeans offer bites.
A moonbeam catches, we dance along,
In this cosmic carnival, we belong.

With every twinkle, joy abounds,
Planetary plays, and silly sounds.
In the vastness, we find delight,
Making memories in the starlit night.

Gravity's Lullaby

In the vastness, where silence reigns,
My hair stands up, but that's just strange.
With candy bars that bob and weave,
I munch on jokes, I dare believe.

The sun winks bright, it's up to its tricks,
As we float by with our cosmic kicks.
My buddy's spilt drink creates a mess,
In zero-G chaos, I must confess.

Jovial whirls turn the night so loud,
With laughter dancing, we form a crowd.
The stars all giggle, they know the spark,
In this weightless world, we leave our mark.

So here we sail on this funny ride,
With every misstep, we cannot hide.
In this celestial dream, let's frolic and play,
For laughter's the treasure that won't fade away.

Zero-Gravity Harmonies

In space we spin and twirl around,
Our giggles echo, a weightless sound.
We dance with stars, our feet in air,
Floating like feathers without a care.

Silly songs float past our ears,
As laughter bubbles, banishing fears.
Cosmic tunes and playful glee,
In this vast void, we're wild and free.

With every twang and plucky beat,
We bounce through space on tippy feet.
A stellar chorus, bizarre delight,
Singing our hearts out in the night.

So join our merry floating spree,
A joyful dance, just you and me.
Together we'll tumble, soar and glide,
In this zero space, we shall abide.

Floating Fragments

Bits of chatter swirl like dust,
In orbits bright, we simply must.
Moons chuckle back with gleaming eyes,
As we craft jokes that touch the skies.

Our sandwiches float, refusing to fall,
While laughter cascades, a cosmic sprawl.
Juicy treats take flight, it's true,
Who knew lunch would become a zoo?

With giggles caught in our tangled hair,
We zero in on fun, laid bare.
The giggly chase through twinkling night,
Is a thrill ride that feels just right.

Every chuckle breaks the bound,
In this zero space, we're unbound.
Fragments of joy float everywhere,
Differences lost in the weightless air.

Galactic Jam Session

In a ship that jiggles, we gather near,
With instruments floating, oh, so clear.
Guitars strum softly, drums lightly bang,
As we play chaos, the stars sang.

Pitching our voices with cosmic flair,
The aliens join in, without a care.
A saxophone squeaks, a trumpet whines,
Creating tunes that blur all lines.

The comet's tail sways to our groove,
As we twist and bounce, together we move.
In this galactic party, all's well,
Together we laugh, all's swell!

Floating rhythms, an endless spree,
Harmony stretches through galaxies.
So let's jam on this celestial ride,
In a universe where fun's our guide!

Beyond the Weight

We laugh in loops, a merry twist,
In this lightness, we can't resist.
Bouncing off walls, what a delight,
No weighty rules to hold us tight.

Our shoes take flight, in playful jest,
With every leap, we float the best.
A wacky race, through stars we speed,
Zero obstacles, just joy and heed.

A necklace of stars around our necks,
Sprinkled laughter, what a complex!
As we tumble through this cosmic haze,
Every moment a brand-new phase.

So here we float, the universe wide,
With silly tricks we cannot hide.
Beyond all weight, we soar and play,
In this grand expanse, forever stay!

Cosmic Connections

In a ship made of cheese, we float with ease,
Chasing stars like kids, caught in a breeze.
Jellybeans drift, under the moon's soft glow,
We giggle and laugh, in the void below.

A cat in a hat, with a space-walk strut,
Chasing its tail, oh what a nut!
Floating past planets, we play peek-a-boo,
Making friends with comets, how d'you do?

A dance with a quasar, what a sight to see,
In cosmic ballet, we're all carefree.
Bouncing off asteroids, what a wild chase,
Zero gravity games in this vast, open space.

Silly space socks, they twirl and spin,
In a galaxy where we all fit in.
Joking with aliens over alien tea,
In this endless expanse, just you and me.

The Void Sings

In the stillness of space, the void hums a tune,
Giggling at meteors that dance like a loon.
Stars twinkle and wink, they join the fun,
In this cosmic playground, there's always a pun.

Gravity's gone, so we leap and we bound,
Echoes of laughter are the best kind of sound.
Planets align, throwing a wild ball,
As we tumble and glide, having a ball.

With a wink and a twirl, our antics unfold,
Cosmic clowns of the night, brave and bold.
Floating through galaxies, sharing a jest,
Finding humor in space, we're truly blessed.

The universe chuckles, its vastness so wide,
As we orbit around, joyously aside.
Let's sing to the stars, let our voices unite,
For the void is a stage, and we shine so bright.

Weightless Reflections

Mirror in space, reflect a big grin,
As we float in a bubble, let the mischief begin.
Giggles spill out, with each flustering spin,
In this airy escape, together we win.

Puppies in spacesuits are barking with flair,
Chasing their tails, without a care.
A dance with a nebula, swirling in style,
Every twist brings laughter; it's our best trial.

Zipping past stars, like a racecar on track,
Hold onto your hats, we won't turn back.
Making faces at rockets, what a funny scene,
In weightlessness, joy is the supreme queen.

Juggling planets, oh what a feat,
Even asteroids join in, tapping their feet.
In the cosmic funhouse, our spirits take flight,
In this endless adventure, everything's right.

Dreaming in Orbit

Drifting through dreams, in a starry embrace,
Floating with laughter, it's a magical race.
The moon whispers secrets, the sun winks with cheer,
Interstellar giggles echo, bringing us near.

A pink unicorn bounces, with flair like no other,
Chasing a star, like a goofy big brother.
Bubbles in space, we're filled with delight,
With every soft pop, we float into night.

Gigantic marshmallows prepare a sweet feast,
Zero-gravity games never seem to cease.
Dancing with stardust, we weave and we sway,
In this dreamlike orbit, we frolic and play.

With smiles that sparkle like stars shining bright,
In this cosmic wonderland, we're wrapped up tight.
Adventures keep growing, with each passing swirl,
In our dreamy domain, let's give it a whirl.

Cosmic Cadence

In space, my socks dance, twirl with glee,
Floating so high, they're wild and free.
Bouncing off walls, they giggle and glide,
A cosmic ballet, on this starry ride.

Asteroids roll, like marbles they spin,
Chasing my dreams, oh where do I begin?
With laughter erupting, we spin round the sun,
In the grand universe, we're all just having fun.

Planets in pajamas, they waltz in a line,
Mischief in orbit, everything's fine.
Gravity's a myth, it seems so absurd,
When comets perform, it's a sight to be heard.

Galactic giggles light up the void,
Where black holes snicker, not once annoyed.
In this laughter-filled void, with all senses aflare,
We float through the cosmos, silliness everywhere!

Starlit Sonnet

Stars do the tango, oh what a sight,
With nebulas swirling, they dance through the night.
Comets play hopscotch, leapfrogging in space,
While aliens chuckle, lost in their grace.

The moon wears a bowtie, so dapper and bright,
While meteors race past, a vivid delight.
Galaxies burst with a bright, jovial spark,
As laughter expands through the vast, endless dark.

Jupiter juggles with rings, like a clown,
While Saturn just giggles, spinning around.
With glee in our hearts, we drift through the air,
In a universe bursting with joyous affair.

Oh what a ride, on this wild cosmic spree,
With friends made of stardust, just you and me.
In this melodious void, where joy has no end,
We twirl through the night, with each starry friend.

Weightless Wordplay

In zero gravity, words start to float,
They giggle and bounce like a playful boat.
Letters make friends, forming words with a cheer,
In this silly world, there's nothing to fear.

Sentences somersault, phrases do flips,
Like astronauts sharing their fun little quips.
A universe crafted in linguistic delight,
Where each goofy sentence takes off in flight.

With commas as spacemen, dashes take flight,
All soaring together in the soft starlit night.
A cacophony of laughter, a symphonic spree,
Creating a melody, so carefree and free.

So toss out your worries and let the fun soar,
In this realm of the playful, we'll all smile more.
With each twist and turn, we craft and we play,
In the absurdity of space, we dance through the day.

Celestial Stanzas

In the cosmos' embrace, we chuckle and sway,
Where stars paint our dreams in a whimsical way.
Space-time giggles, such a cosmic delight,
As we spin and we twirl through the silvery night.

Cosmic critters play tag on the rings of a star,
While black holes are hiding, oh so bizarre.
With laughter as fuel, we dance without care,
In this orbiting playground, floating through air.

The sun tells a pun, making planets all grin,
While asteroids join in with a wink and a spin.
Each twinkling light shares a jest or a tease,
As we float through the ether, completely at ease.

So come take a ride where the universe laughs,
With joy in our hearts, let's fill up our glass.
For in this grand ballroom of cosmic delight,
We'll dance with the stars until the dawn breaks bright!

Poetic Orbital Paths

In a ship made of cheese, we float and we twirl,
With gravity gone, we dance and we swirl.
My sandwich drifts by with a laughable grace,
As I chase it through this fantastic space!

Bananas do flips, while I giggle with glee,
My cat learns to sail in a place so carefree.
The stars wink at us with a playful delight,
As we bounce off the walls, what a funny sight!

A pencil does cartwheels, it jots down a jest,
While we sip on some juice, feeling ever-so blessed.
Floating and bouncing, oh what a grand spree,
In the galaxy's playground, we laugh endlessly!

With moon pies for lunch and Earth tunes in our ears,
We sing to the void, fueled by cosmic cheers.
In this wacky expanse, our giggles ignite,
Creating a symphony, oh what a delight!

A Symphony of Stars

Each star plays a note in a cosmic parade,
As comets all dance in a glimmering cascade.
We spin with the music, a baffling ballet,
Where the laws of physics just decide to play!

With Neptune on drums and Mars on guitar,
Venus weaves harmonies, never too far.
The Milky Way sways in a jazzy refrain,
As we clap with our feet, enjoying the gain!

A black hole's a trumpet, a wild crazy sound,
While asteroids join, their rhythm unbound.
The laughter expands like the universe wide,
As we groove in the silence, oh what a ride!

So let's sing with the stars, let's brighten the night,
In this space of wonders, our hearts take flight.
In the lead of the cosmos, we dance and we sway,
Creating a symphony that's here to stay!

Celestial Conversations

Two planets began to exchange a few words,
Discussing the joys of their orbiting birds.
From Saturn's bold rings to Jupiter's stripes,
They share all their tales with comical gripes.

A meteor jumps in with a story to tell,
About crashing on Earth and the wonders as well.
The planets all chuckle, their laughter a stream,
As the meteor blushes, or so it would seem!

"Oh dear, I was messy!" the stardust did snort,
As asteroids howled in a jovial sport.
With twinkling eye beams, they set off the fun,
As cosmic companions, there's no need to run!

So let's gather around in this joyful embrace,
Sharing stories of giggles with stars in the space.
What a wacky assembly, a humorous spree,
In the laughter of galaxies, wild and free!

Dreams on the Edge of Gravity

Floating in dreams, I take flight with a grin,
Where the laws of our world lose their strict, silly spin.
Through clouds made of candy, I tumble and sway,
In this whimsical realm where I giggle all day!

A trampoline's waiting at each cosmic skip,
I bounce off the moon with a joyous flip!
With rockets for shoes and stars for my hat,
I leap like a bunny, just look at me—fat!

The sun's a big smile, the comets all cheer,
As dreams take their shape, and my mind shifts gear.
With laughter that echoes through glittering space,
I dance through the void, wearing stardust with grace!

In this edge of the cosmos, where silliness reigns,
I forget all my troubles, dance away all my pains.
With dreams in my pocket and a twinkle in eye,
I soar through the universe, oh me, oh my!

Echoes of the Infinite

In space so wide, we spin in glee,
Lost in the stars, just you and me.
Weightless giggles float through the air,
As we wobble 'round like we haven't a care.

Galactic pies we toss and share,
With zero gravity, what a fine affair!
Asteroids bounce like a rubber ball,
Laughter echoes through the cosmic hall.

A comet's tail just tickled my nose,
I'm dodging planets, oh, how it goes!
With meteors dancing, we join the spree,
In this silly realm, we're so carefree.

Shooting stars make wishes that we can't catch,
While spinning in circles, we have a good match.
In the silent void, our chuckles resound,
Making music of madness, joy unbound.

Floating Poetics

Words drift like feathers, all over the place,
In cosmic flotillas, we find our space.
Floating verses, they twist and twirl,
As we spin in joy, what a silly whirl!

The universe giggles with each little blip,
While rhymes do cartwheels, they join the trip.
A quasar's wink is a funny surprise,
Like jokes in the air, they dance through the skies.

Stardust confetti falls down like rain,
We gather it up, what a colorful stain!
Life in the cosmos, all glitter and cheer,
With light-year puns, we banish the drear.

Astro-balloons bob in playful glee,
Making us chuckle, just wait and see!
Inscribed on a planet, our fun we'll declare,
In this wacky void, we'll spread it everywhere.

Cosmic Reflections

Looking in mirrors made of light,
I see my face, oh what a sight!
Fluttering around like a starry sprite,
Two-space giggles ricochet, oh what delight!

Invisible strings pull us near,
As we tumble through space with no fear.
Reflected laughter fills up the void,
With echoes of voices, hilarity employed.

Floating like bubbles, we bounce all around,
Attracting the laughter, the silliest sound.
Whirling in orbit, who's dizzy today?
In this cosmic fun, we laugh all day.

With each twist and turn, the fun multiplies,
Caught in this cosmos, where humor defies.
We ride on the waves of celestial jest,
In the infinite skies, we'll never rest.

Lyrical Lightyears

Boundless lines stretch across the expanse,
As we journey through planets, a whimsical dance.
Galaxies swirl with their colorful hues,
While we chase the laughter, we sing our own tunes.

Comets rush by with a wink and a grin,
In this cosmic bubble, let the fun begin!
We flip through the stardust, a playful delight,
As visions of giggles take off in flight.

Meteors whiz past, like jokes on the wing,
And the laughter erupts from the joys that we bring.
In space all alone, we're never confined,
With each burst of joy, our worries unwind.

We barter with time, like it's nothing at all,
Floating on rhythms, that cosmic ball.
A blend of absurdity wraps us in cheer,
In this vast universe, we shed all our fear.

Celestial Flight

In the vast of space, we take a leap,
With giggles and glee, it's quite a sweep.
Stars twinkle bright, our laughter ignites,
Floating like feathers on whimsical nights.

Asteroids dance in a comical way,
As we twirl and spin, come what may.
With zero gravity, our jokes take flight,
Silly faces painted in pure delight.

Bouncing off planets, we're free as can be,
Gags echo loudly, just you and me.
In this cosmic comedy, we find our place,
A joyful adventure through the vast space.

With zero rules, we float and we play,
Creating our laughter every single day.
In the heart of the cosmos, so bold and spry,
We tickle the stars as we zoom by.

Verses Beyond the Vortex

Spinning through space like a merry-go-round,
Our laughter's the fuel for the fun that we've found.
With each silly bump, our spirits soar high,
In the whirlwind of giggles, we laugh 'til we cry.

The planets join in with a whimsical cheer,
As we stumble and fumble, there's nothing to fear.
Meteor showers shower us with delight,
Grinning with glee in the deep velvet night.

In orbits of chuckles, we glide through the air,
Chasing our shadows without any care.
With scintillating puns, our minds intertwine,
In this vortex of joy, all perfectly fine.

So here's to the cosmos, our playful retreat,
Where the jokes float along, and laughter's a treat.
With hearts filled with humor, we'll journey afar,
Creating our verses among shining stars.

Floating Verses

In a bubble of wonder, we drift and we glide,
With a pinch of silliness, our laughter won't hide.
Gravity's out, and whimsy's in play,
Tickling the cosmos in a playful ballet.

Wobbling fiercely on a comet's bright tail,
We concoct our own tales, we're giggling pale.
Across cosmic highways, we chuckle and spin,
Finding joy in the chaos, where do we begin?

Our smiles float freely, like bubbles of glee,
In this galaxy's dance, it's just you and me.
With verses like rockets, we blast into space,
In this funny adventure, we find our own grace.

Through the laughter of stars, we'll forever explore,
The humor in nothing, the joy we adore.
So let's toast to the void, a celestial cheer,
In the absence of weight, our fun's crystal clear.

Gravity's Lyrical Embrace

In the arms of the void, where we chuckle and sway,
We giggle with planets that playfully stray.
Dancing like raindrops, we float in the air,
Where each starry wink brings an improv flair.

Comics of cosmos, our routine's ever bold,
With punchlines to chase, our humor unfolds.
We spin like a top, in joy we engage,
While writing our stories on gravitation's page.

With each twist and turn, we stifle a laugh,
Juggling variables like a mathematical craft.
Orbiting laughter, our smiles ignite,
In this zany adventure, everything's right.

So here's to the moments that cause all the cheer,
In a universe playful, our hearts persevere.
May our playful embrace always brighten the skies,
With giggles and grins, we'll reach for the highs.

Freefall Poetry

Up in the sky, I float and twirl,
My pen escapes, gives flight a whirl.
Words drift like stardust, what a sight,
Laughing with comets, it's pure delight.

A quirk of physics, a word's ballet,
Watch it giggle and bounce, hooray!
No gravity here, just joy on the fly,
With every stanza, we dance and glide.

Floating away, my thoughts take aim,
Chasing moonbeams, it's all a game.
Jokes in space, a cosmic play,
In this wacky void, we laugh all day.

So pen your dreams with glee in tow,
Let every verse in silence flow.
With humor afloat, let spirits soar,
In this weightless world, who could ask for more?

Astro Aria

In the stratosphere's hug, we laugh and sigh,
Each chuckle expands like a bubble in the sky.
Notes of mirth tumble, like spacey confetti,
Compose your giggles; oh, aren't we ready?

Waltzing with satellites, twirling with stars,
This goofy ballet escapes earthly bars.
Gravity's gone, we're giddy as kids,
Creating absurdity, spinning our lids.

A cosmic cartoon, out of control,
Tickling the universe, heart and soul.
With every quip, we leave our trace,
In this endless void, we find our place.

Sing to the void, let your laughter ring,
In the ballet of life, just let your heart sing.
With echoes of joy, we'll craft our song,
In this galactic dance, we'll always belong.

Celestial Cadence

Stars snicker softly, a glittering jest,
Spinning our tales in the cosmic quest.
Dancing through silence, our chuckles align,
In the grand universe, we're simply divine.

Floating in rhythm, no tether in sight,
Galactic giggles are pure, what a flight!
Rainbow-colored echoes bursting like glee,
In this fanciful realm, we roam wild and free.

Each verse is a rocket, igniting our minds,
Witty little wonders, a treasure one finds.
In the laughter of stardust, we weave our delight,
Our celestial symphony plays through the night.

So jot down the whimsy, let spirits take wing,
From the farthest reaches, the funny will spring.
With a chuckle and twirl, we dance with the sun,
In this absurd universe, we're forever young.

Dreaming Among the Stars

In dreams we tumble, through cosmic sea,
Twinkling chuckles float, oh so free!
With each little giggle, we sway and spin,
In this silvery dance, let the fun begin.

Asteroids giggle, planets join in,
Creating a chorus, where to begin?
Stars chuckle back, as we bounce and glide,
Through the vastness of space, our joy can't hide.

So write it all down, be merry and bright,
In this whimsical world, we burst like starlight.
Floating in laughter, no worries to keep,
In this grand little universe, let's take a leap!

With each funny thought, we travel afar,
In dreams, we find joy, like a shooting star.
Breaking all bounds, on this humor spree,
Among the bright stars, we laugh endlessly.

Weightless Whispers

In a ship where dreams take flight,
We're bouncing like balls, what a sight!
Floating snacks, oh what a treat,
Watch that sandwich, it's off your seat!

Galactic giggles fill the air,
Zero gravity, without a care.
Jellybeans dance, stars twirl around,
In this cosmic fun, joy abounds!

Catch a comet, oh what a ride,
With my space suit, I'm filled with pride.
We'll race the sun, it's a madcap chase,
Orbiting laughter all over the place!

Asteroids bounce like rubber balls,
In this lightness, nobody stalls.
So come join us, let spirits soar,
In this wacky space, you'll never be bored!

Interstellar Interludes

Galactic shenanigans in full view,
We're flipping and flopping, just like goo.
Unruly astronauts, in orbit we spin,
Lost in a whirl, let the fun begin!

With a twist of the hips, we float through the door,
Chasing each other, it's never a bore.
A rubber chicken flies past my head,
In this bouncing ballroom, it's all about tread!

Dancing with planets, we kick up a fuss,
Gravity's lost, not making a fuss.
In the Milky Way, we twirl and we glide,
With laughter and tricks as our cosmic guide!

So hold on tight to your cosmic drink,
It might just float off, who'd ever think?
In this stellar romp, we've got not a care,
Just some funny friends in the great dark air!

Spacebound Sonnets

Rockets zoom with a bumpy cheer,
A cosmic circus, my oh my dear!
Wobble and jiggle through starry scenes,
Banana peels float like silly machines.

Astronaut antics, oh such a show,
Spinning in orbits, come join the flow.
Waves of laughter echo through time,
In this great expanse, all jokes can rhyme!

With asteroids bouncing in a carefree spree,
Who knew space travel could be so zany?
Flip-flops and laughter, a jolly affair,
In the great beyond, we haven't a care!

As we glide through the cosmos, a comic ballet,
You'll find gravity's jokes lighten the way.
So grab your space buddy for fun and cheer,
In this galaxy grand, all's merry and clear!

Beyond the Atmosphere

Past the clouds where the rockets zoom,
We're off to explore the galactic room.
Where giggles and chuckles reign supreme,
In this universe, we'll chase a dream!

Floating high, there's no need to rush,
In a weightless world, we'll join the hush.
Catch a bubble, give it a poke,
Laughter erupts, what a funny joke!

With planets that giggle and moons that jive,
Our laughter echoes, so alive!
Starry friends dancing without a care,
In this cosmic waltz, we happily share!

So strap in tight, let's take off in glee,
For out in the stars, we are wild and free.
A funny adventure, a stellar spree,
In the vastness, it's just you and me!

Melodies from the Milky Way

In a spaceship made of cheese,
The astronauts dance with ease.
Jupiter sings a silly song,
While Saturn joins, it won't be long.

Galaxies laugh with a twinkling light,
Comets play tag, a wondrous sight.
Nebulas giggle, clouds all around,
Space is a playground, fun to be found.

Stars waddle and dip in delight,
Zero gravity makes them take flight.
A cosmic ballet with laughs in the air,
Every twirl spins laughter, joy everywhere.

From Pluto to Mars, the fun won't cease,
A cosmic circus, a merriment feast.
As the cosmos chuckles, we float on by,
In laughter we soar, reaching for the sky.

Astral Alliterations

Silly satellites spin and sway,
While meteors munch on Milky Way.
Galactic giggles in a starlit spree,
Float and frolic, just you and me.

Wacky worlds whirl in wobbly moves,
Asteroids dance to the vibes and grooves.
Planets pop with playful wit,
In space, no worries, we'll never quit.

Cosmic chuckles, a zany scene,
Floating through dreams, it's all so serene.
Twinkling tunes from the stars align,
In funny verses, we sip space wine.

Laughter echoes through the dark void,
In this vast realm, we're overjoyed.
With every spin, a joke takes flight,
In this galactic, giggly night.

Stringing Stars Together

Twinkling treasures, a string of light,
Connect the dots, oh what a sight!
Cosmic crafts from stardust sway,
Hitch a ride on the Milky Way.

Jokes on Mars, they're flinging far,
Venus laughs at the silly bazaar.
Uranus spins with a grin so wide,
In a joyful float, we take a ride.

Stringing stars, a necklace bright,
In a festival where mirth ignites.
Laughing black holes and comets in race,
Space wraps us up in a playful embrace.

Galactic giggles echo around,
In laughter's orbit, joy is found.
We knot these stars with a charm so clever,
In the cosmos of humor, we float forever.

The Poetry of Planets

Planets prance in a joyful trance,
With each little bounce, they take a chance.
Earth tells jokes, and Mars cracks up,
Mercury spins with a bubbly cup.

Venus giggles, her humor contagious,
In this cosmic play, it's quite outrageous.
The sun shines bright, with a wink, it beams,
Painting the sky with our funniest dreams.

Dancing through space, oh what a trove,
A melody woven in giggly groves.
With every twist, the stars unite,
In the poetry of planets, we feel the light.

So come join the fun, let's float away,
With laughter and play, we'll seize the day.
In this vast universe, all fears unwind,
In the happy void, true joy we find.

Celestial Symphony

In space, my socks do float around,
A dance of fabric, bliss profound.
Gravity took a break today,
As my snacks drift slowly away.

I tried to juggle snacks up high,
But peanut butter flew awry.
With cosmic giggles, I do see,
My lunch has made a birdie flee.

My pet fish spins, a dizzy blur,
As he confuses space with fur.
A bubble forms, then pops with glee,
The vacuum keeps on laughing free.

Each star above is just a wink,
As we all gather 'round to think.
Why don't we twirl and laugh a bit?
In this wild void, we just commit.

Fragments of the Cosmos

Stardust sprinkled on my head,
Makes for a very comfy bed.
I spin and giggle, float with ease,
As meteors graze my frozen knees.

An asteroid's a bouncing ball,
Its roundness makes me laugh and fall.
I catch it like a silly whale,
With my cosmic partners, we set sail.

Banana peels drift by my side,
In this weightless world, what a ride!
A comet comes, gives me a shove,
I zoom past planets, oh so in love!

The vacuum sings a cheerful tune,
While I dance with stars and swoon.
Moonbeams tickle my toes so light,
In this playful space, all feels right.

Verses in the Void

Floating freely, my hair's a mess,
As I orbit marshmallows, I confess.
My cereal spills like tiny moons,
In this giggle fest, I hum silly tunes.

A space cat hovers near my head,
Purring softly, it makes my bed.
As zero-g lifts us high and low,
We twirl like dancers, making a show.

With stardust sprinkles, popcorn flies,
As I reach for snacks with starry eyes.
Jokes echo loudly, the void does cheer,
An interstellar party, my friends all near.

In the vastness, I feel so bold,
With laughter and fun, here's my gold.
Each moment floats like a feathered kite,
Spreading joy in the endless night.

Cosmic Quatrains

Atop a comet, I take a seat,
With candy bars I plan to eat.
A squirrel astronaut gives me a grin,
Together we whirl, let the games begin!

Stars blinking bright, they wink at me,
As I swing with grace like a cosmic tree.
With giggles and joy, I jump and slide,
In this silly dance, I take great pride.

Space does a flip, then tumbles around,
When I let loose, I am unbound.
The rockets roar, a fitting song,
In this universe, where we all belong.

So grab your friends, let laughter soar,
In this galactic dance floor.
Where fun and humor chase away strife,
In the boundless void, we celebrate life!

Intergalactic Verses

In spacesuits we dance, so odd, so light,
Floating like socks that took off in flight.
We giggle and wiggle, with glee so profound,
In the cosmic ballet, we're lost and unbound.

Invisible music plays on a whim,
Singing through silence, our voices get dim.
But laughter's contagious in stellar embrace,
As we spin and twirl in this wacky vast space.

Our snacks are tacos that float in a whirl,
Each bite is a game, watch the salsa unfurl.
We savor the flavors in weightlessness grand,
Like astronauts munching on food from a can.

So cheers to the cosmos, where humor takes flight,
We're comedians dancing through the starry night.
A universe filled with jokes round and bright,
Together we'll laugh, 'til all's out of sight.

The Sound of Silence in Space

In the vastness where whispers go to hide,
We shout at the void, let our gibberish slide.
Echoes are tricky, they play peekaboo,
Yet we crack up at nothing, laugh a hullabaloo.

Stars keep their secrets, they twinkle and tease,
While we float on our backs, enjoying the breeze.
With a pun here and there, our shuttle turns gay,
In the quiet abyss, we find things to say.

A bubble of humor floats straight to the moon,
With giggles aplenty, we dance to our tune.
No gravity here, just pure joy and jest,
In silence we find that the fun is the best.

So let's dip our toes in the void's endless cup,
A galaxy's worth of chuckles, fill up!
Here in the stillness, our laughter takes form,
An odd kind of music, with space travel warm.

Beyond Boundaries

Past the meteors, where the comets do race,
We glide like balloons, having fun in this place.
With jokes about aliens, we giggle with glee,
Imagining green folks having tea by the sea.

Each star is a wink, a playful decree,
That fun knows no limits, it's wild and so free.
Gravity's got nothing on laughter's sweet thrill,
As we soar with the planets, our spirits just spill.

Cosmic connections, we weave in our flight,
Tickling stardust with humor so bright.
Beyond all the boundaries, we float side by side,
In this circus of wonders, we joyfully glide.

So step into orbit, where smiles take lead,
In this endless expanse, we've all that we need.
With chuckles that soar and hearts that expand,
We'll make fun of the galaxy, hand in hand.

Harmonies of the Cosmos

In this weird symphony of stars up above,
We create our own rhythm, all laughter and love.
Bouncing through space like a rubbery tune,
The galaxies jiggle; we're over the moon!

Our voices collide in a jubilant dance,
Like particles swirling in cosmic romance.
With silly sound bites that echo just right,
Mirth is our mission, shining so bright.

With the moons as our stage and the sun as the light,
We perform our best acts every starry night.
Interstellar chuckles will drift with the breeze,
While we share our creations, just glowing with ease.

So here in the cosmos, we're free to explore,
In harmony's laughter, we always want more.
A giggle, a snort, let the universe hear,
With humor and joy, there's nothing to fear.

www.ingramcontent.com/pod-product-compliance
Lightning Source LLC
Chambersburg PA
CBHW070751220426
43209CB00083B/866